Contents

CU00731003

How to use this guide

Most of the pages look like the one shown on the right. Each page shows a site or object as it looked in Roman times, with red labels highlighting key points of interest. Blue squares show parts of Roman sites you can see in the present day. Each page also has a map showing the site or object's present day location and how to visit the site.

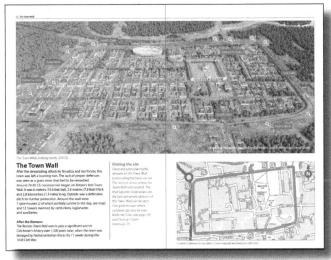

Roman Colchester looking north, 200 CE.

Introduction

Colchester has a long and complex history, spanning thousands of years. For example, stone axe heads have been found in Culver Square that are almost 10,000 years old. But arguably Colchester is most well known for its extensive Roman history, including the devastating attack by Boudica. This guide explores the period from 43 CE to 200 CE. After this date the Roman Empire started a gradual decline and by 410 CE Britain was under constant attack by marauding Anglo-Saxons.

The guide brings to life how Colchester could have looked, with full-colour images all looking north *(unless specified otherwise)*, illustrations of contemporary people and detailed maps showing where each site is in present-day Colchester.

Evolving archaeology
This guide aims to give an impression of how these sites and objects could have looked in Roman times.
Two of the sites mentioned in this guide, the amphitheatre and the basilica, have not yet been found. It is generally agreed that Colchester would have had them, but where exactly they were located is still unknown. As more sites are uncovered our understanding of Roman Colchester will change.

The Romans

The city of Rome in central Italy was formed around 800 BCE and grew over the centuries into the Roman Empire, which covered most of Europe and northern Africa. It was a highly sophisticated and technologically advanced society, with a huge army, major roads and large cities.

Britain at that time was a mysterious place with fierce tribes and valuable metals, which became the focus of an attempted invasion in 55 BCE and 54 BCE by Julius Caesar.

Those invasions were repelled by local tribes and the Romans did not try again to invade Britain for almost 100 years.

By 43 CE the Emperor Claudius *(who needed the senate and army's support)* decided to invade Britain, which was weakened by the death of King Cunobelin of the Trinovantes, who lived in Camulodunum *(Colchester)*.

Gathering his forces, Claudius set his sights on Colchester...

Visiting Colchester
Colchester lies about 50 miles north-east of London.
There are two main museums which show Roman Colchester in depth:
Colchester Castle Museum in the town centre and the Roman Circus Visitor Centre (a short distance south of the town centre).
Extensive remains of the Roman Town Wall and partial remains of other Roman sites can also be seen.

Coin mint of Cunobelin

Unloading imported goods from the Roman Empire

Metal working sites

Farmstead

Farmland

Outline of present day Colchester town centre

Colchester, looking north, 30 CE.

Camulodunum

The area which is now Colchester was part of a significant settlement called Camulodunum*. The centre was located at Gosbecks a few miles to the south-west of present day Colchester and was ruled by King Cunobelin until he died around 40 CE.

It was an area of great importance when the Romans invaded in 43 CE. The invasion force was led by the Emperor Claudius, with thousands of soldiers and possibly elephants. After the successful invasion of Camulodunum, the Romans needed to establish a permanent base of operations.

They chose the present day location of Colchester as it was close to the centre of Camulodunum and to a reasonably sized river, allowing goods to be imported.

*Camulodunum is the Roman name for Camulodunon which meant the fortified place of Camulos (the Celtic god of war).

Visiting the site

Camulodunum covered a huge area, most of which is longer visible. Colchester Castle Museum (blue square) has artefacts such as coins and weapons that show what life was like before the Roman invasion of 43 CE. The area nearest the town centre was the equivalent of an industrial area, producing coins and other artefacts. This is shown with a red dot on the map and main image. The dotted red line shows the outline of the present day town centre.

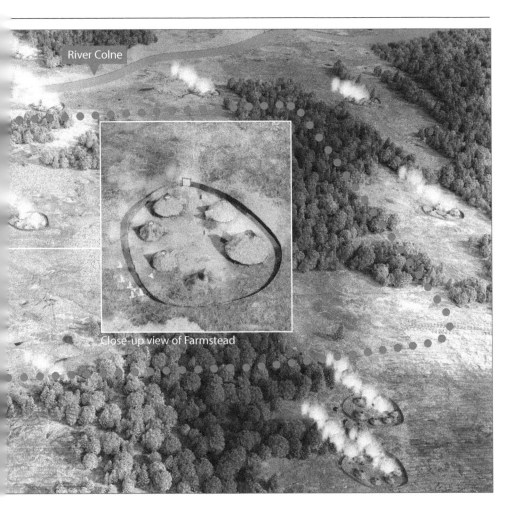

River Colne

Close-up view of Farmstead

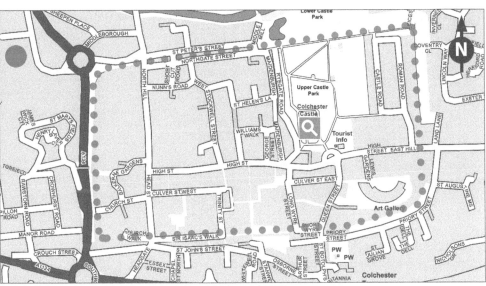

Site of the Legionary Fortress, looking north, 48 CE.

The Legionary Fortress

In 44 CE a fortress was constructed in the south-west corner of the present day town centre.

The main units that built the fortress were the 20th Legion and an auxiliary unit from what is now present-day Bulgaria. The fortress had a ditch system to protect it from attack, with wooden walls for extra security. Inside were *Praetentura (barracks)* to house all the legionaries as well as the *Principia (administrative building)*. The *Legatus legionis (a rough equivalent of a general)* occupied the *Praetorium*.

Here matters such as how the army would be deployed were discussed.

Unusually, the fortress *(the first of its kind in Britain)* had an annexe, which may have contained baths and stores for the army. It seems as though the fortress was never fully completed, as it was soon to become a city.

Visiting the site

There are no visible remains of the Roman fortress (red lines). Artefacts used in the fortress such as weapons and armour can be seen in Colchester Castle Museum (blue square). The dotted red line shows the outline of the present day town centre. The main image also shows a close-up view of one of the entrances into the fortress, with legionaries (soldiers) marching out on patrol.

Tents

Annexe

Defensive ditch

Close-up view of South Gate-house

Outline of modern day Colchester town centre

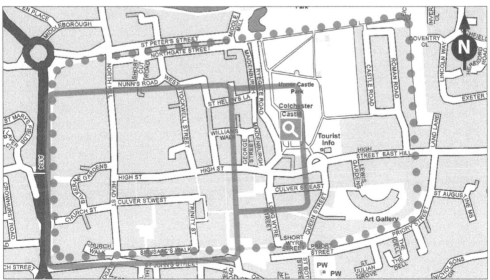

Labels on image: Triumphal Arch · Repurposed Principia · Repurposed Praetentura · Filled-in defences

Colonia Victricensis, looking north, 58 CE.

Colonia Victricensis

Around 49 CE, due to unrest in Wales, the legions needed to be redeployed. The fortress that was still unfinished instead became a colony. Its purpose was to show the native Britons what it meant to be *'Roman'*, with huge public buildings such as the Temple of Claudius, the Theatre and a Triumphal Arch celebrating Claudius's victory. The colony was called *Colonia Victricensis (roughly City of Victory).*

This may be where the name *Colchester* came from originally. At first the buildings of the fortress were repurposed into housing and then the rest of the town plan was laid out in grids. The original defences of the fortress were filled in to make more space. This lack of defences and the fact that the native Britons were forced to pay for the construction of the town was to cost the Romans dearly, just a few years later.

Visiting the site

Some of the present day streets follow the original Roman Street plan, such as the High Street and North Hill/Head Street (blue squares). As the city grew, more streets were added in the north-east and east. The dotted red line shows the outline of the present day town centre. Other sites from this time include the Temple of Claudius and the Theatre (blue squares).

Theatre

Temple of Claudius

Outline of modern day
Colchester town centre

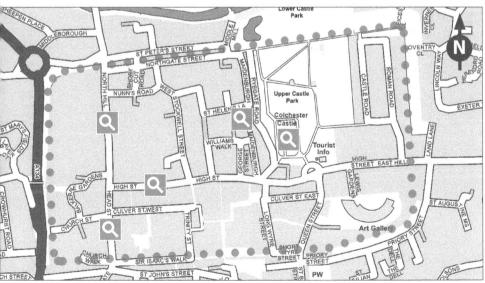

Contains Ordnance Survey data © Crown copyright and database right 2022

Triumphal Arch

Fenwick Treasure

No Town Wall

Filled-in outer ditch

Site of Boudica's attack, looking north, 60/61 CE.

Boudica destroys Colchester

In 60/61 CE the Iceni *(a tribe that ruled the area roughly covered by Norfolk)* mounted a rebellion against the occupying Roman forces. The Iceni led by Queen Boudica* swept south gathering around 120,000 warriors, including people from the local Trinovates tribe.

Their first target was Colchester, which at the time had a small garrison of around 500 Roman soldiers and possibly a few thousand ex-soldiers.

The Iceni burned the town to the ground and centred their hatred on the Temple of Claudius. The towns-people and soldiers made a last stand sheltering inside the temple.

The Ninth Legion attempted to retake the town but were forced to flee. In the end the town was left a burning ruin as Boudica and her forces moved south towards London.

There are different spellings of Boudica/Boudicca/Boadicea that have been used since Roman times.

Visiting the site

Archaeologists have found a burn line (called the Boudican destruction layer) covering large parts of Colchester. There are artefacts on display in Colchester Castle Museum (blue square) which date from the Boudica attack, including food which was preserved by the intense heat of the huge fire. The Fenwick Treasure (blue square) also dates from the attack by Boudica and her forces. More about the Fenwick treasure is shown on page 26.

Temple of Claudius

Boudica's forces

Outline of modern day Colchester town centre

eatre

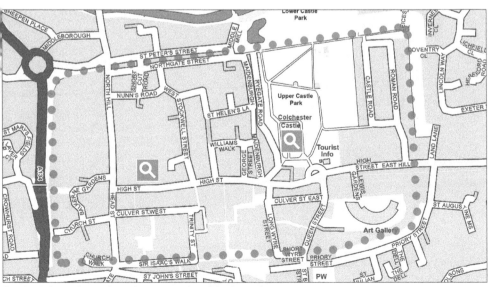

The Town Wall, looking north, 200 CE.

The Town Wall

After the devastating attack by Boudica and her forces, the town was left a burning ruin. The lack of proper defences was seen as a gross error that had to be remedied.
Around 70-85 CE construction began on Britain's first Town Wall. It was 6 metres *(19.6 feet)* tall, 2.4 metres *(7.8 feet)* thick and 2.8 kilometres *(1.5 miles)* long. Outside was a defensive ditch for further protection. Around the wall were
7 gate-houses *(2 of which partially survive to this day, see map)* and 12 towers manned by centurions, legionaries and auxiliaries.

After the Romans
The Roman Town Wall was to play a significant part in Colchester's history over 1,500 years later, when the town was besieged by Parliamentarian forces for 11 weeks during the 1648 Civil War.

Visiting the site
There are extensive visible remains of the Town Wall surrounding the town centre. The red line shows where the Town Wall was located. The blue squares show where the best preserved sections of the Town Wall can be seen.
Two gate-houses which survived can also be seen: Balkerne Gate (see page 14) and Duncan's Gate (see page 16).

Duncan's Gate

East Gate

South Gate

Outer ditch

Note, the locations of the Amphitheatre and Basilica are conjectural.

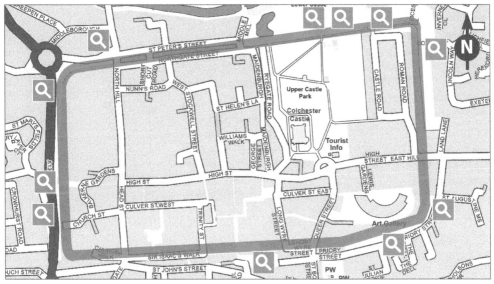

CREEPEN PLACE

MIDDLEBOROUGH

ST PETER'S STREET

MIDDLE MILL

Lower Castle

INVERON CL

LICHFIE

N

NORTHGATE STREET

NORTH HILL

NUNN'S ROAD

WEST STOCKWELL STREET

ISHORT CUT ROAD

MAIDENBURGH

RYEGATE ROAD

CASTLE ROAD

ROMAN ROAD

LINCOLN WAY

HERE FORD

EXETE

ST HELEN'S LA

Upper Castle Park

Colchester Castle

ST MARY'S FIELDS

LAYER

WILLIAMS WALK

GEORGE STREET

MAIDENBURGH

Tourist Info

HIGH STREET EAST HILL

LAND LANE

BLACKERAE GARDENS

HIGH ST

HIGH ST

HEAD ST

CULVER ST WEST

GEORGE STREET

CULVER ST EAST

LEWIS GARDENS

ST AUGUSTINE MS

A83

CROWHURST ROAD

CHURCH ST

TRINITY ST

LONG WYRE STREET

QUEEN STREET

Art Gallery

RIORY STRE

THE

OAD

CHURCH WALK

GATE

SIR ISAAC'S WALK

SHORT WYRE STREET

PRIORY STREET

THE DELL

UCH STREE

ST JOHN'S STREET

ST BO

STRE

PW

ST JULIAN

NOL SONS

Contains Ordnance Survey data © Crown copyright and database right 2022

Site of Balkerne Gate, looking east, 200 CE.

Balkerne Gate

A Triumphal Arch to Emperor Claudius had been constructed before the Town Wall was built. This was placed on one of the main entrances into the town connecting it to London. It had two arches, an inscription *(possibly to Claudius)* and a quadriga* on the top of the structure.

After the Town Wall was built the arch had to be incorporated into the main western gate-house *(Balkerne Gate)*, which made it more difficult to defend than a standard gate-house. There was an aqueduct nearby which was used to transport water into the town.

Balkerne Gate was probably blocked up around 300 CE due to increasing raids by the Anglo-Saxons.

*A Quadriga is a sculpture of four horses, found on many Triumphal Arches.

Visiting the site

There are visible remains (blue square) next to the A134 (Balkerne Hill) of part of the gate-house, although there are no visible remains of the Triumphal Arch. The site is connected to some of the best preserved sections of the Roman Town Wall (red line on map) to the north and south. The site lies just to the west of the High Street and is dominated by a red brick Victorian water-tower called Jumbo.

Aquaduct

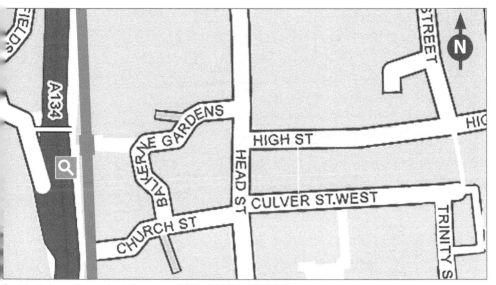

Site of Duncan's Gate, looking south, 200 CE.

Duncan's Gate

The only other gate-house to survive to the present day is Duncan's Gate. It is named after Dr PM Duncan, who in 1853 discovered the gate-house with its single passageway into the town. The main image also shows how the Town Wall was a continuous circuit so that troops, such as auxiliaries, could move to any part rapidly. At the end of each street or at a corner there were guard-towers which would be used as observation posts.

Combined with the defensive ditch the Town Wall made the town much easier to defend.

The fate of the other Gate-houses (see page 12)

North Gate was demolished in 1823. East Gate collapsed a few years after the Civil War of 1648.

Headgate was the site of a fierce battle during the Civil War and was demolished by 1766. South Gate was demolished in 1814.

Visiting the site

There are visible remains of the gate-house (blue square) just outside Upper Castle Park. They are connected to some of the best preserved parts of the Roman Town Wall to the north-east (red line).

Lower Castle Park hosts many concerts and fairs throughout the year. Upper Castle Park lies just north of the east end of the High Street, behind Colchester Castle.

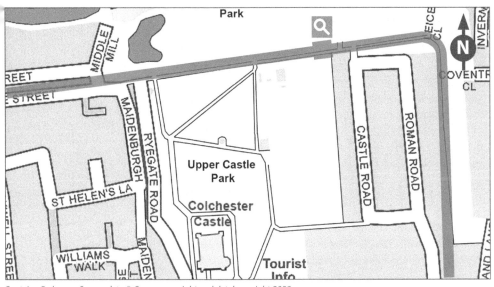

Site of the Temple of Claudius, looking north, 200 CE.

The Temple of Claudius

Around 54 CE a large temple was built, dedicated to Emperor Claudius and standing over 20 metres *(65 feet)* tall. It is the largest Roman temple found in Britain.

It was the centre of the Imperial Cult, in which the Emperor Claudius was worshipped as a god, although construction of the temple might not have started until after his death in 54 CE. The temple was badly damaged during the attack by Boudica and her forces in 60/61 CE *(see page 10)*.

Around 80-100 CE an arcade was built around the temple. This would have enclosed a sacred area where only a select few such as Imperial priests were allowed.

After the Romans

Around 1000 years after the temple was built, Colchester Castle was built around the ruins of the temple. Colchester Castle is the largest Norman keep in Britain.

Visiting the site

Most of the Temple and arcade was repurposed for building material after the Roman period. The best remains can be seen on a tour of Colchester Castle vaults. The vaults are actually the base of the temple's podium. The castle (blue square) is now a museum which features a detailed history of Colchester, with extensive Roman artefacts and reconstructions on display. Colchester Castle is at the east end of the High Street.

Roman Arcade

Temple of Claudius

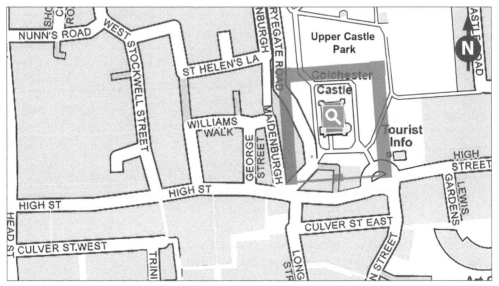

Contains Ordnance Survey data © Crown copyright and database right 2022

Magistrates' box

Seating for 8000 spectators

Water basin

Starting gates

Entrance

Turning post

Site of the Roman Circus, looking north, 200 CE. The town can be seen in the distance.

The Roman Circus

In 2004 the only known example in Britain of a Roman Circus was discovered. It would have been nearly 450 metres *(1476 feet)* long and around 72 *(236 feet)* metres wide. Built some time in the 2nd century it would have seated over 8000 people. The Roman Circus was used to host chariot races, which were popular in Roman times. Each race started at the western starting gates with eight charioteers. They would race down the south side of a water filled basin and turn at each of the turning post columns. Whoever completed seven laps first and crossed the finish line was the winner. The races were often extremely dangerous, with the charioteers taking great risks to win. Judges at the finish line declared who had won, while nearby a special box was situated for sacred objects to *view* the races. Magistrates also watched over the races at the starting gates to ensure the races were run correctly.

Visiting the site

Large amounts of the Roman Circus, which occupied a huge area, have now been built over. The best preserved section is of the starting gates (blue square). The starting gates can be seen at the Roman Circus Visitor Centre, which features a detailed history of Roman Colchester and the Roman Circus. The Roman Circus Visitor Centre is a short walk south of the town centre, off Butt Road. (For Sat Nav use the postcode CO2 7GZ).

Cult box

Main entrance

Racing chariot

ish line

Lap counter

Turning post

Judges' box

Market stall

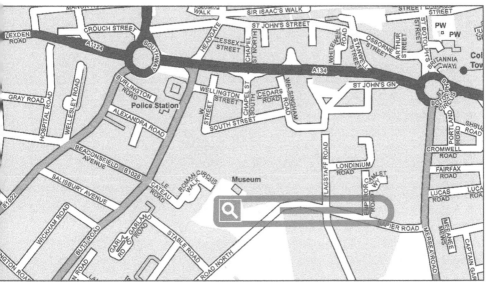

Site of the Roman Theatre, looking north, 200 CE.

The Roman Theatre

A large Roman theatre was discovered in Maidenburgh Street, which would have been able to seat at least 3,000 people. Pantomimes were more popular than plays, as well as comedies based on people's lives.

The audience would have entered the theatre through the *Vomitorium* and sat in the semi-circular *Auditorium*, overlooking the *Orchestra (stage)*.

The theatre was mentioned by Tacitus *(a Roman historian)* as being one of the buildings in Colchester at the time of Boudica's attack. This theatre was probably rebuilt on the site of the original theatre destroyed by Boudica and her forces. The building would have stood over 20 metres *(60 feet)* tall with a large and complex stage area including the *Scaenae frons*, which was full of columns and provided a background for the actors.

Visiting the site

Most of the theatre was lost hundreds of years ago. There are visible remains on Maidenburgh Street, which lies off the High Street. Part of the outline of the theatre is marked on the street, along with a large archaeological reconstruction of the theatre by Peter Froste.

The blue square on the map and main image shows where the surviving part of the theatre can still be seen.

Scaenae frons

Auditorium

Orchestra

Vomitorium

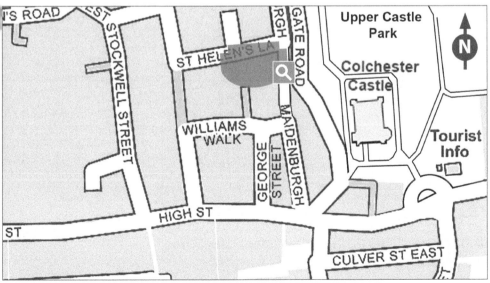

Site of the Roman Town-house, looking north, 200 CE.

The Town-house

In Upper Castle Park lies the ruined tessellated floor of a Roman town-house. The inhabitants would have been quite wealthy and lived in the *Pars Urbana (living area)*.
The *Pars Rustica* was where the slaves and cook worked, while the *Villa Fructuria* would have been used as stores for the whole house, such as food products. The house would have been large by today's standards, with a water supply, heated floors and roof tiles. Rooms in the Town-house included: the *Triclinium (dining room)*, the *Tablinum (study)*, *Culina (kitchen)* and the *Vestibulum (entrance hall)*.

Interpreting the site

Archaeologists have found evidence of three houses in this area; here two of the three are shown. Working out exactly when a structure was built can be very difficult. Some of the techniques used to date a structure include: historical records, carbon dating and how deep in the soil it is.

Visiting the site

There are visible remains of part of the flooring of the Town-house (blue square) in Upper Castle Park, which lies behind Colchester Castle. Parts of the Roman Town Wall can also be seen, just north of the Town-house (shown with red lines on the map).

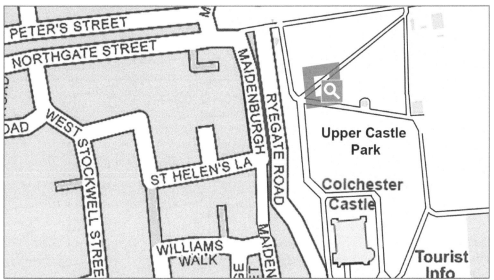

Contains Ordnance Survey data © Crown copyright and database right 2022

Some of the woman's jewellery found at the Fenwick store, dating from around 60/61 CE.

The Fenwick Treasure

During the attack on the town by Boudica and her forces *(see page 10)* a wealthy couple who lived in Colonia Victricensis desperately hid their treasure. If they escaped is not known, but the treasure did survive.

It was discovered in 2014 during renovations to the Fenwick department store, on the High Street. The jewellery was hidden under the floor of a rich family house which was destroyed after the attack. The jewellery consisted of many pieces including gold and silver ear-rings, necklaces and finger rings. The woman who owned the jewellery most likely had slaves and might have been the wife of a veteran soldier. Roman women visited the theatre, shops, temples and the baths, but were not allowed to vote.

Other activities they might have enjoyed included visiting the chariot races, and some even travelled across the Roman Empire.

Visiting the site

There is a small exhibition about the jewellery inside the Fenwick department store (blue square) on the High Street. At the time of writing the jewellery is in the British Museum, London.

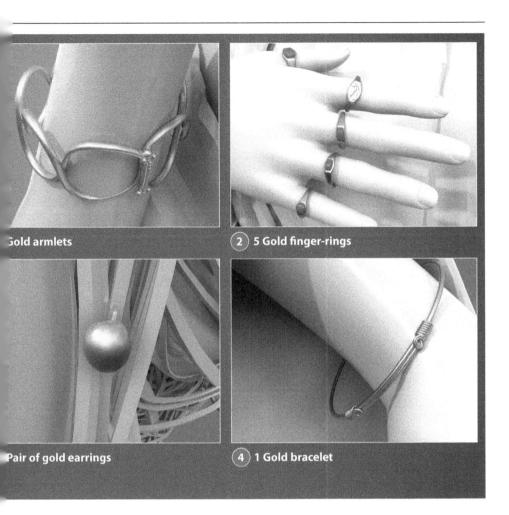

Gold armlets

(2) 5 Gold finger-rings

Pair of gold earrings

(4) 1 Gold bracelet

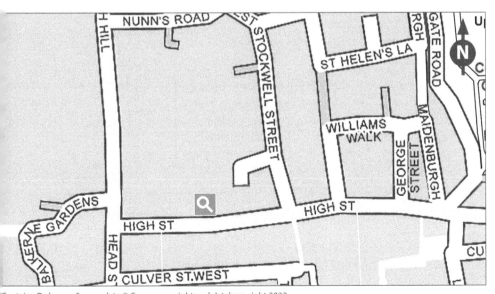

Site of the Bathhouse, looking north, 200 CE.

The Bath-house

As Britain's first capital city, Colchester had many public buildings, including a Bath-house. Recently remains which are possibly part of a public Bath-house were found near to Colchester Castle *(see map)*. It would have had a furnace to heat the *Caldarium (hot room)* and the *Tepidarium (warm room)*. There was also a *Frigidarium (cold room)* and *Palaestra (exercise area)*. The men and women would have bathed in their own areas where people could socialise, in some ways like our present day swimming pools. The Romans did not have soap products, so instead used oil and scraped the oil off with a curved implement called a strigil. *(An example is on display in Colchester Castle).*

The remains that were found here were possibly a replacement Bath-house built after the attack by Boudica in 60/61 CE. The original might have been built at the same time as the Roman Fortress.

Visiting the site

There are no visible remains of the possible location of the Bath-house (marked in red on the map). It is thought to be located at the junction between the High Street and Long Wyre Street.

Frigidarium

Tepidarium

Caldarium

Palaestra

Furnace

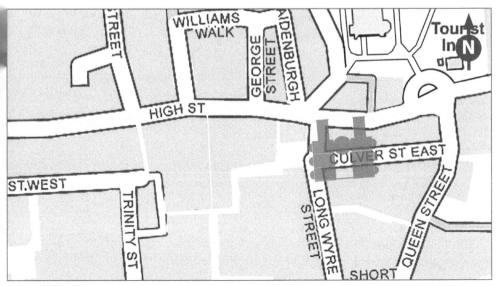

Lectus tricliniaris

Glassware

Samian ware bowl

Possible interior of the town-house which housed the Berryfield mosaic, 200 CE.

The Berryfield Mosaic

In 1923 a market gardener unearthed a mosaic floor dating from around 200 CE in his garden, where the *First Site* building now stands. The mosaic would have been located in a grand town-house's *Triclinium (dining room)*. Here the owner would have entertained guests, possibly wealthy merchants or politicians. Inside the *Triclinium* there would have been ornate furniture such as *Lectus tricliniaris (lounges)*, blue glassware and fine foods*.

Other mosaic floors have been found around Colchester such as North Hill and Culver Square. Some of these can be seen in Colchester Castle.

*Colchester Castle has many examples on display of glassware, pottery, Samian ware and food. The food, such as dates and figs, was burnt and had become carbonised. This happened during the attack by Boudica in 60/61 CE.

Visiting the site

The Berryfield mosaic is displayed inside the First Site building (blue square) at the east end of the High Street. First Site is an award winning art gallery with exhibits, cafe and many events throughout the year.

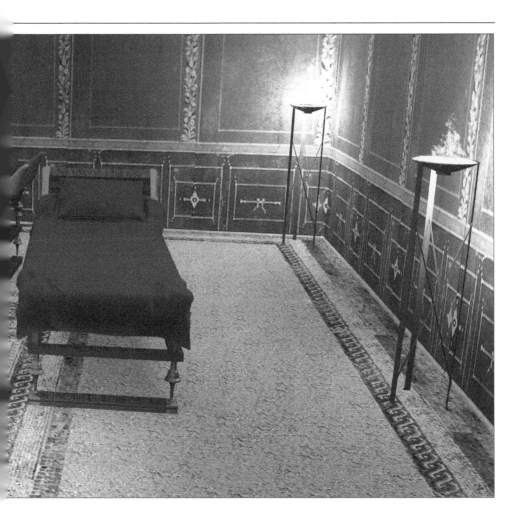

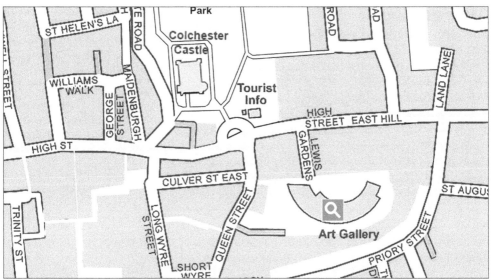

Possible site of the Basilica, looking north, 200 CE.

Government offices

The Basilica

Colchester would have had a Basilica and it **may** have been located near to Colchester Castle *(see map)*.

The Basilica was the commercial and administrative heart of Colonia Victricensis. While ordinary people were not permitted into the Temple of Claudius and the arcade, the Basilica was where deals were made and laws practised. The Romans had a highly sophisticated legal system which underpins civil law practised in modern times.

Large statues would have dominated the *Forum (public square)* where the population of the local area could meet. Surrounding the forum were various offices for local administrators and merchants. There would probably also have been market stalls selling food and household items sourced from all over the Roman Empire. Some of this would have been transported in large amphorae *(pottery containers)*, which can be seen in Colchester Castle.

Visiting the site

There are no visible remains of the Basilica (marked in red on the map), which is thought to be at the east end of the High Street, opposite Colchester Castle. It is now the site of the Natural History Museum, with exhibits about local wildlife and more.

The Visit Colchester Information Centre is also nearby, in the Georgian Hollytrees building (blue square).

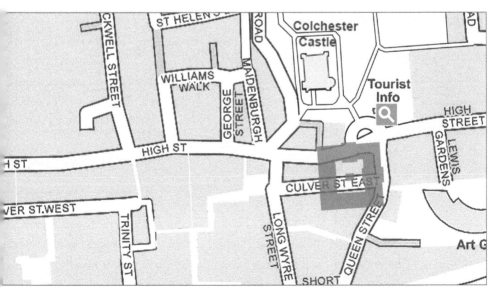

Possible site of the Amphitheatre, looking south, 200 CE.

The Amphitheatre

A city as important as Colonia Victricensis would have had an amphitheatre. Although at the time of writing no structure has been found, it **may** have been located where shown. The amphitheatre would have been a large building seating thousands of people, all wanting view of the gladiators fighting. There would have been a sophisticated system to protect the crowds *(but not the gladiators)* from the sun called a *velarium*. The *vomitorium* were the entrances and exits used throughout the amphitheatre.

Shops and stalls would have been clustered around the base of the amphitheatre, selling food to the crowds.

Contests often began with the gladiators *(Latin for swordsmen)* paraded in front of the crowd, with music playing. These contests often started in the morning, with the victors celebrated in the middle of the day.

Visiting the site

There is a debate about the exact location of the Amphitheatre (marked in red on the map). At the time of writing one possible location could be at the end of West Stockwell Street, off the High Street. This area of Colchester is known as the Dutch Quarter and features many fine buildings. It is also where Ann and Jane Taylor lived, who wrote the famous rhyme 'Twinkle, Twinkle Little Star'.

Vomitorium

Velarium

Seating

Gladiators

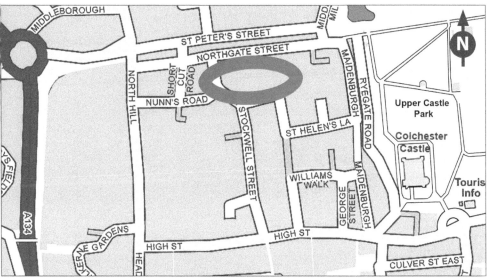

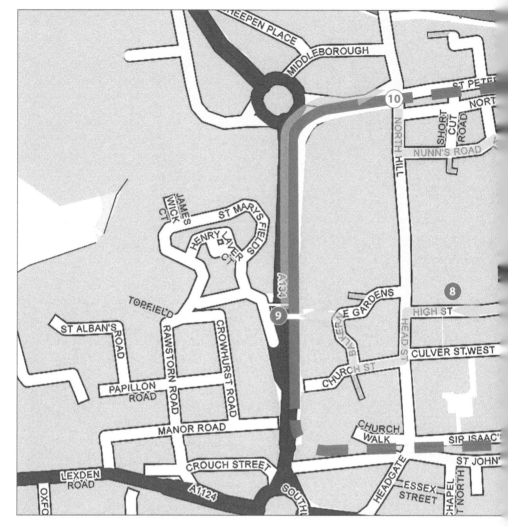

A short walk around Roman Colchester

This is a short walking tour around some of the sites shown in this guide. The tour is wheelchair and buggy friendly and is estimated to take under an hour.

There are two excellent museums which have Roman artefacts, Colchester Castle and the Roman Circus. Colchester Castle is located just off the High Street and the Roman Circus is 20 minutes walk from Colchester town centre at Roman Circus walk, off Butt Road.

Note the locations of the Amphitheatre and Basilica are conjectural and based on the models at the Colchester Archaeological Trust.

Symbols used on this map

▬ Route of short walk

▬ Town Wall
(Still visible, see page 12)

▪▪ Town Wall
(No longer visible)

③ Roman site/object
(Still visible)

④ Roman site
(No longer visible)

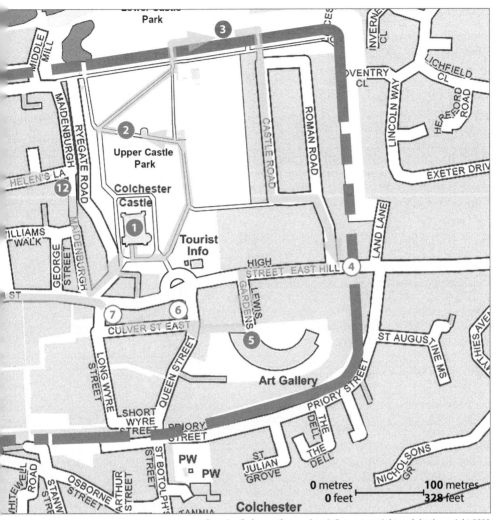

Contains Ordnance Survey data © Crown copyright and database right 2022

First published March 2022
ISBN 978-1-3999-1697-4 *(Paperback)*
First Edition

Designed and published by JC3DVIS
www.jc3dvis.co.uk
Book design © 2022 Joseph Chittenden

All the images in this guide were produced by JC3DVIS.
Contains Ordnance Survey data © Crown copyright and
database right 2022
Certain images contain CC BY-SA 3.0 images
(see website for details).

With special thanks to:
Colchester Archaeological Trust Phillip Wise
Jane Chittenden
Peter Froste
Phillip Taylor

Legal disclaimer
Neither the author nor the publisher shall be held liable or
responsible to any person or entity with respect to any loss
or incidental or consequential damages caused, or alleged to
have been caused, directly or indirectly, by the information
contained herein.

Lightning Source UK Ltd.
Milton Keynes UK
UKHW020408210722
406077UK00006B/245

9 781399 916974